THE UK
WORLD ADVENTURES
BY HARRIET BRUNDLE

BookLife

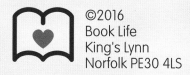

©2016
Book Life
King's Lynn
Norfolk PE30 4LS

ISBN: 978-1-910512-64-7

Written by:
Harriet Brundle
Edited by:
Grace Jones
Designed by:
Matt Rumbelow

A catalogue record for this book
is available from the British Library.

THE UK

WORLD ADVENTURES

CONTENTS

Words in **bold** can be found in the glossary on page 24.

THE UNITED KINGDOM

The countries England, Scotland, Wales and Northern Ireland together make the United Kingdom (UK).

SCOTLAND

NORTHERN IRELAND

WALES

ENGLAND

Each of the four countries has their own capital city: London, Edinburgh, Cardiff and Belfast.

LONDON, ENGLAND

EDINBURGH, SCOTLAND

CARDIFF, WALES

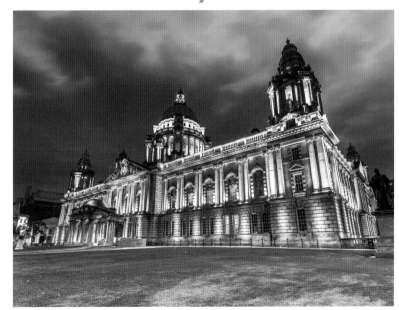

BELFAST, NORTHERN IRELAND

WHERE IS THE UK?

The United Kingdom is an island, which means it has water all around the land. The UK is near to France, Germany and Spain.

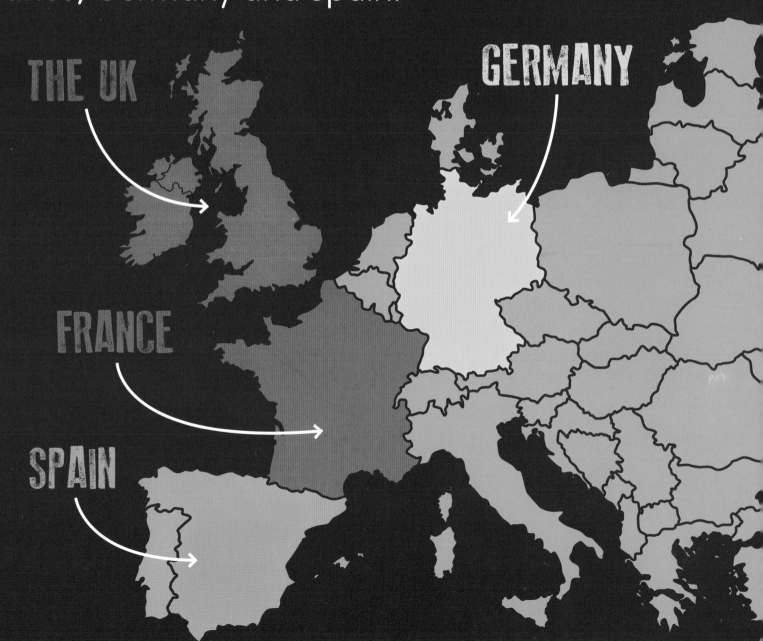

THE UK

GERMANY

FRANCE

SPAIN

The Union Jack is the flag of the United Kingdom, but each of the four countries that make the UK also have their own flag.

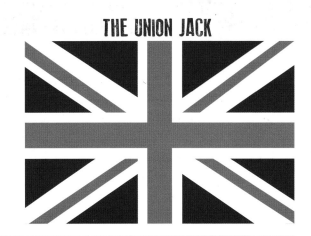

NORTHERN IRELAND

SCOTLAND

WALES

ENGLAND

WEATHER AND LANDSCAPE

The United Kingdom is mostly warm in the summer time and cool in the winter. The UK does not usually have any **extreme** weather.

There are lots of different landscapes in the UK.
Some parts have hills and others are very flat.
The UK also has many coastal areas.

NORTHERN IRISH COAST

SCOTTISH MOUNTAINS

CLOTHING

The UK does not have a **traditional** style of clothing in day-to-day life but on special **occasions** like weddings, it is traditional for the bride to wear a white dress.

People from lots of different cultures live in the United Kingdom and so many different styles of clothing are worn.

RELIGION

The religion most popular in the UK is Christianity but many different religions are also followed, including Hinduism, Islam and Sikhism.

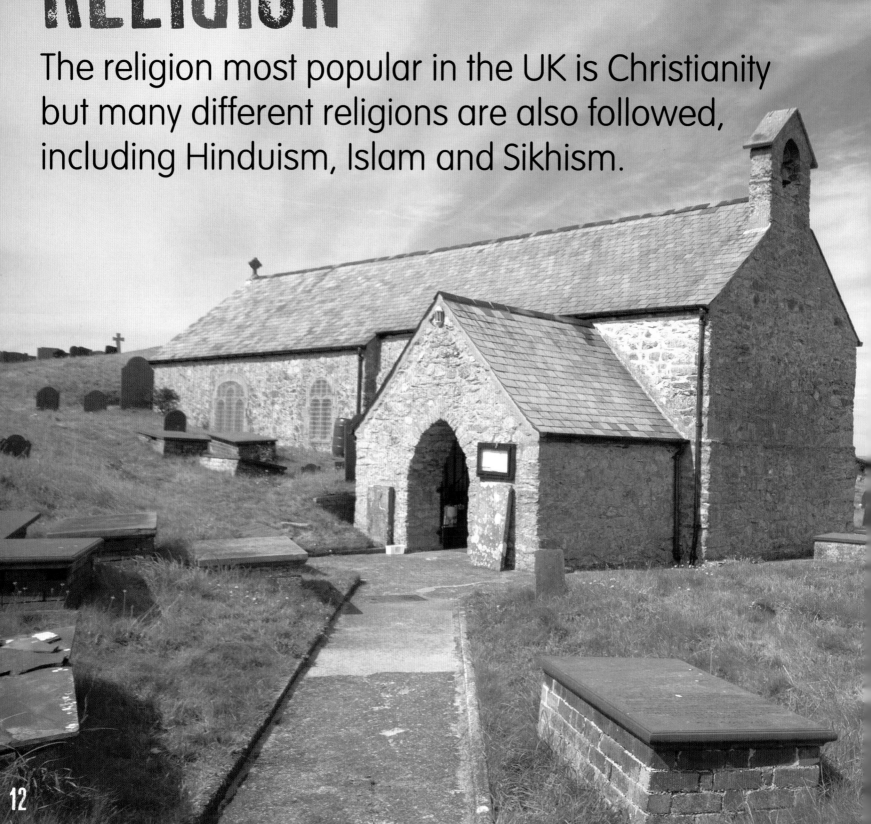

Christians celebrate many events throughout the year, including Easter and Christmas. At Christmas, a tree is usually decorated and gifts are given.

Many people in the UK do not follow any religion.

FOOD

Each of the four countries in the UK has their own traditional dishes. One traditional English meal is fish and chips.

A traditional dish in Scotland is called haggis, which is made from sheep heart, liver and lungs. The dish is usually eaten with potatoes.

AT SCHOOL

Children in Wales, Scotland and Northern Ireland must go to school until they are 16 years old. In England, children must go to school or college until they are 18 years old.

Children in the UK learn lots of different subjects, including maths and science.

AT HOME

The cities in the UK are much busier than the towns and villages. The cities have sky scrapers and some people live in high tower blocks.

In towns and villages, houses are usually less **modern**. One traditional style of home is a thatched house. The roof is made from straw and reed.

SPORT

In 2012, the Olympic Games were held in London. The UK won a total of 65 medals in sports such as cycling, tennis and rowing.

It is thought the most **popular** sport in the UK is football. Other sports such as cricket and rugby are also very popular.

FUN FACTS

The Queen of the UK owns one-sixth of the whole of Earth's land.

The oldest house in the UK is 6,000 years old.

There are over 30,000 people with the name John Smith in England.

John Smith

If you live in the UK, on your 100th birthday the Queen will send you a birthday card!

GLOSSARY

extreme: something very good or very bad

modern: something that has been made using recent ideas

occasion: special event

popular: liked by lots of people

traditional: ways of behaving that have been done for a long time

INDEX